Shadruchulu

A journey of love, loss, and flavours

Words by Deepthi Tanikella
Art by Mounica Tata

INDIA · SINGAPORE · MALAYSIA

ISBN

Hardcase 979-8-89929-297-2
Paperback 979-8-89673-755-1

The significance of Ugadi Pachadi is immense as it symbolises the essence of life, as it has all the tastes of life. It teaches that life is a mixture of all the emotions. When put together, these tastes are known as **Shadruchulu**.

These stories are from my life experiences. I have tried to stay true to the essence of the memories; however, the writer in me sometimes took a slightly offbeat path by adding my views. Here is my tribute to all tastes of life.

Dedication

To my Amma, Chilukuri Nagaraja Lakshmi, the lioness whose hands built my world, whose food and words carried love, and whose absence I now fill with flavour and memory: You roar in every spice, every simmering pot, and every story I tell.

My father, Tanikella Suri Babu, taught me the poetry of food and the quiet strength of presence. I imagine him cooking with Bheema and Nala, debating life and verse with Sri Sri Garu in that eternal kitchen.

To my brother, Tanikella Sethu Vijay, whose laughter echoes in every moment I recreate from childhood. Club 27 holds your fire, and I carry it forward.

To Vinod Chandramouli, my partner, through years of love, laughter, lessons, and everything. Thank you for always holding me. 'Together' is the word I truly learned from you.

And to Vivaswath, Vedavyas, Vasishta, and Katyayani, my little moons and sun, you are the heartbeat of my days, the laughter in my kitchen, and the reason I create, remember, and dream.

To Rocky and Shiro, you teach me to be selfless and mostly grab treats when given without being shy!

This book is for all who find comfort in food, remember home with every bite, and keep stories alive through cooking.

Contents

Preface

This book was born out of a deep yearning to savour the flavours of the past, hold on to the memories of those I've lost, and preserve their stories through food, which is the only way I know how. In my parents' kitchen, food was more than just a means of sustenance; it was a language of love, remembrance, and quiet understanding. They believed every meal carried its own poetry, that the right combination of flavours could tell a story without words.

My brother taught me that the most beautiful moments are often found around the table, the clacking of steel plates, the shuffle of flavours, and the comforting silence of a meal cooked with care.

When I lost them, I reached for recipes to cook and remember. I wanted to relive the aroma of my mother's pappu on the stove, the crisp bites of my father's favourite kandabachali, and the dishes my brother and I fought over on the table. With every stir, every taste, and every carefully measured spice, I felt them return, even if only for a moment.

This book is a tribute to the hands that fed me, the voices that shaped me, and the love that continues to nourish me, even in their absence.

It is also a book for my children's future so that they will know the flavours of home, the stories of their people, and the comforts of tradition. This book is dedicated to

Vinod, my lifelong companion, who constantly reminds me that love, like food, thrives best when shared.

And for you, dear reader, wherever you are, whether trying to recreate the taste of home, discovering something new, or simply searching for a familiar story, may you find warmth in these pages, a memory in every recipe, and a piece of yourself in every bite.

Teepi / Sweet

My parents used to write letters to each other while they were engaged to be married; I have a treasure trove of those letters. This series of letters was our favourite one, as Nana[1] taught Amma[2] to cook. Years later, they would compete for the best Sunday Lunch cookathon.

---

1 Nana - Father in Telugu

2 Amma - Mother in Telugu

Suri sat at his desk in the small bank in his remote village in Telangana, staring at the blank sheet of paper in front of him. He had promised Lachi, the woman he was set to marry in just a few months, that he would write to her every day until their wedding. They had decided to follow this tradition to keep the excitement alive in the months leading up to their union.

Suri laughed as he picked up his pen to write to Lachi. “You won’t believc what happened at the bank today,” he wrote. “I was sitting at my desk, in the middle of some paperwork when a herd of cows just waltzed in.”

“I mean, actual cows!” Suri wrote. “I think they wandered in from the nearby field. I tried to shoo them out, but they, yes, the cows looked at me like I was crazy.”

“But wait, it gets better,” Suri continued. The farmer who came to ask for the loan to extend his cow shed yesterday got the cows to prove that he had no place for them anymore! So he left them in the bank and just walked out! Imagine the chaos that the bank was in!

Forever yours,
Suri

Lachi burst out laughing. “I can’t even imagine what that must have been like,” Lachi couldn’t help but feel grateful for Suri’s letters. Even though they were apart, they could still share their lives in the most meaningful way. And the thought of Suri dealing with a group of cows and the farmer in the middle of his workday made her love him all the more.

Lachi, on the other hand, wrote about her job as a sales executive for the Omo company. She told Suri about the products she was selling, the challenges she faced, and the successes she had achieved.

"Dear Suri," she wrote,

"I want to live peacefully with no targets, nothing for the next few months. You know I've applied for a job at Nana's office, and I am 100% sure I am getting it; I've always been good at numbers. Nana thinks the idle mind is the devil's workshop, so when the letter came from this company, he told me to work smart, earn money, and save it up.

Amma has been teaching me how to cook. The other day, she asked me to make Rasam, and I boiled tamarind and water and added salt and chilli powder; that is how Rasam is made, right?

Amma was flabbergasted and was going on about how I would live in a house like yours with five brothers and three sisters and not know what to do in the kitchen!

I told her, *Amma, I will go to work, and Suri will also be at work, and when we come back, we will hire a cook or come here to eat.*

She was in tears; you should have seen her that night; I think I've given her a migraine.

Okay, I am tired now, ta-ta.

Lachi."

Suri's heart skipped a beat as he read her words. "Don't worry, my love," he wrote back. "I'll teach you everything I know. And who knows, maybe we'll discover some new recipes together."

Suri wrote, "Lachi, I can't wait to marry you and spend the rest of my life with you. I want to cook you my favourite dish, Payasam, and share it with you under the stars."

Lachi smiled as she read his words. "Oh, Suri, you always know how to make me smile," she wrote. "But you know I don't know how to cook. I'm afraid I won't be able to cook anything for you."

Suri was called to a meeting, and he silently added a reminder to make Payasam that night and write the steps so that Lachi could surprise her family by making it.

Suri finished work and returned home, where he lived with his two friends who worked in the same bank. They loved having him as a housemate. Suri made delicious food and had the knack of elevating any recipe.

"Suri, what's cooking tonight?" asked Murthy. "I am making Payasam today," said Suri. "Payasam? Isn't that for dessert? We were asking what is the main course," Hanu clarified. Suri told them why he wanted to make Payasam that day, and the three men went straight to the kitchen and started cooking up a storm.

Lachi handed her father her salary and asked him if she could keep 25 rupees with her. "Why do you need the money?" her father asked. She wanted to tell him that it was her hard and smart-earned money. But, before she could say that, he said, "This is your money. You could have kept the Rs. 25 and given me the rest."

"Never ask for what is yours if it is rightfully yours, Lachi," he said and gave her Rs. 25.

Lachi wrote, "Suri, my father is a large-hearted, kind man; I hope and pray that you are the same. Otherwise, we will be in trouble right from the word go. Oh, I have to go now to buy the ingredients," she said, leaving the letter on her table and heading to the grocery store.

"Now, Lachi read this part; it is crucial; it makes or breaks your dish. Your mood when cooking has to be calm and happy; your mood reflects in the food, passing those positive vibes onto the person who eats that food," wrote Suri. "Last night, the Payasam turned out so well that we all ate that for dinner!"

"I remember learning how to make this when I was six. Amma was in the hospital and asked Nana for something sweet. Nana went home and asked our neighbour to make something sweet. I was surprised that Nana did not know how to cook! I thought everyone knew how to. I asked Nana, *Why don't you make it for Amma?* He looked at me, laughed and said, *Me, a man, cooking and making merry in the kitchen?* At that point, I did not understand what he was saying. But I remember lying to Amma and telling her that Nana made the dish; she was so upset.

She was upset that he had to do this for her and started worrying about what others would think. *It will be our little secret,* she said.

When the neighbour's auntie made dinner for us, I asked her, *Aunty, why don't men cook?* She turned around and asked me, *Who said men don't cook? Remember Bheema from Mahabharata? He was an excellent cook. Also, the sweet you love, Mysore Pak, a man invented that.* She held my hand and asked me, *Would you like to cook?* I said yes.

I don't know why. But I remember thinking that I must learn to cook.

Bamma[3] then taught me how to make Payasam, and a month later, I made it for my Amma. Lachi, you must've seen her face; it was beaming with pride. She asked, *Suri, why did you do this for me?* I told her, *Amma, I see you sitting in the kitchen and cooking for all of us, and I want to cook for you, to see you eat first.* Amma decided that day that all her children would learn how to cook. She had five boys after me, and we are experts in the kitchen."

Lachi closed the letter and walked towards the kitchen; she saw her mother and her sisters-in-law making dinner, and her father and her brothers were in the hall reading the newspaper and listening to the news on the radio. She was furious and decided that day, "In our house, every family member will be treated equally."

She wrote the same to Suri in her following letter. "Suri, we will never fight about who does what in our home; you

---

3 Bamma - Paternal Grandmother

cook, and I'll clean, and then some days, I will try to cook for you. But remember, we will be equal in the house."

Suri was delighted to read these words; he always questioned the patriarchal norms and was scolded at home by his father. But his mother taught him the value of equality. Clad in her nine yards, she was far wiser than his father, who was a college professor.

Suri and Lachi's letters became more personal as the weeks went by. They shared their deepest fears and secrets, their hopes and dreams. Suri wrote about his love for Lachi and never feeling this way. Lachi wrote about her admiration for Suri, his hard work, and his dedication to his job.

Finally, the day arrived for Suri and Lachi to meet in person. Suri had been eagerly waiting to cook Payasam for Lachi to show her how much he loved her. But when they met, Lachi surprised him. She had learned how to make Payasam and had made it for him.

Suri and Lachi's eyes met as they sat down to eat, and they both knew that they were meant to be together. Their letters had brought them closer and had allowed them to open up to each other in a way they never thought possible.

From that day on, Suri and Lachi have tried to write letters to each other every day, even after marriage. They knew their words were more than ink on paper; they were a way to express love and strengthen their bond. As they grew old together, they continued to read each other's letters, reliving the memories and moments they had shared.

22/08/75'
Dear Lachi,
cows! can you
They just
This
cows
Forever yours,
Suri

Rice Payasam Recipe

Ingredients

- 1/4 cup of raw rice (or substitute with basmati rice)
- 1 litre (4 cups) milk
- 1/4 cup sugar (adjust to taste)
- A few strands of saffron
- 1/4 tsp cardamom powder
- 1 tbsp chopped mixed nuts (optional, for garnish)
- 1 tsp rose water (optional)

Instructions

1. **Prepare the Rice:**
    - Soak 1/4 cup of raw rice in enough water to fully submerge it. If basmati ricc is uscd, soak it for 30 minutes for a better texture.
    - Rinse the rice two to three times to remove excess starch, then drain and set aside.

2. **Prepare the Milk:**
    - Pour 1 litre (4 cups) of milk into a large, heavy-bottomed pot. Bring it to a rolling boil over medium heat, stirring occasionally to prevent burning.
    - Once boiling, simmer the heat. Scrape the sides of the pot to collect the malai (milk cream) and stir it into the milk. Let it simmer for 5 minutes.
3. **Cook the Rice:**
    - Add the soaked and drained rice to the simmering milk. Stir immediately to prevent the rice from sticking to the bottom.
    - **Stovetop Method:** Cook on low heat, stirring occasionally, until the rice is tender and easily mashed with a spoon.
    - **Pressure Cooker Method:** Transfer the mixture to a tall pressure cooker. Add a small plate or spoon to prevent spillage, then cook on medium heat for 2–3 whistles. Turn off the stove and allow the pressure to release naturally. Check if the rice is tender by pressing it with a spoon.
4. **Sweeten and Flavour:**
    - Once the rice is cooked, mash it slightly with the back of a spoon for a creamier texture.
    - Add 1/4 cup of sugar and stir until fully dissolved.
    - Sprinkle in a few saffron strands and 1/4 tsp of cardamom powder. Mix well to evenly distribute the flavours.

5. **Simmer to Perfection:**
   - Allow the Payasam to simmer on low heat, stirring occasionally to prevent sticking. As it cooks, continue to scrape the sides of the pot and mix the malai back into the Payasam.
   - Simmer until the mixture thickens slightly. Remember, the Payasam will thicken further as it cools, so turn off the heat while it is still a bit runny.
6. **Add Finishing Touches:**
   - Stir in one tsp of rose water (if used) for a delicate floral note.
   - Garnish with one tbsp of chopped mixed nuts. For added flavour, toast the nuts with ghee before sprinkling them on top.
7. **Serve:**
   - Serve the Rice Payasam warm or chilled, depending on your preference. The warm version is comforting, while the chilled version is a delightful treat for hot days.

Tips

- For a richer taste, use full-fat milk.
- If the Payasam thickens too much after cooling, add a splash of warm milk before serving to loosen the consistency.
- Adjust sugar levels to suit your taste.

Enjoy this creamy, flavourful dessert as a special treat or during festive occasions!

Pulupu / Sour

This is a tribute to my brother, who passed away at the age of 27. My father lost his whole self, and my mother refused to be happy again. While on a vacation to Puerto Rico, I stumbled upon a café with "thank you" written in every language in the world. My husband and I wrote it in Telugu and Tamil, and a friend wrote it in Kannada. After returning home, I took my parents to lunch and told them about this beautiful place. We also spoke about my brother and his love for everything life offered.

Savouring the Sourness of Life

It was a rainy evening in Bangalore, and the streets were deserted. The sound of the raindrops hitting the pavement echoed in the silence of the night. A man was sitting in front of the fireplace in a luxurious apartment, staring at the flames with a blank expression. He was Sethu, a famous chef who had lost his only daughter in a car accident a few months ago.

His wife, Smrithi, walked into the room and sat beside him, placing her hand on his shoulder. “Sethu, you need to talk to someone. You can’t keep bottling up your emotions like this. It’s not healthy.”

“I know, Smrithi. But I just can’t seem to find the strength to move on. Whenever I think of cooking, I only remember how much our daughter loved it. And the one dish she loved the most, I’ve never been able to make it for her,” Sethu said, his voice barely above a whisper.

Smrithi looked at him with sadness in her eyes. “I know it’s hard, but you must find a way to honour her memory. Maybe if you go away for a while, clear your mind and find yourself, you can cook that dish for her.”

Sethu shook his head. “I don’t know, Smrithi. I don’t think I can leave the restaurant. It’s the only thing that’s keeping me sane.”

"I understand that, Sethu. But you need to take a break. You've been working non-stop since she passed away. You need to find some peace of mind, and you'll find the heart in you to cook that dish for her."

Sethu sighed and looked at his wife. "I'll think about it."

Sethu looked at Smrithi and asked her, "What about you, Smrithi? How are you facing grief? How are you so strong?"

Smrithi looked at him and smiled. She said, "I don't remember the last time I smiled, Sethu; I don't remember enjoying something and feeling at peace. But I made a promise to myself to honour her, to honour her memory. I often think of cutting myself, hurting this very body that gave birth to her. I am doing everything in my bones to keep her memory alive. You know, I write things that I would want to do with her. That helps me; it feels like I am talking to her."

They both hug and cry. They weep so loudly that their pet, their daughter's best friend Shiro, joins in and howls. The three of them wail in misery until exhaustion finally gives way to sleep.

Sethu woke up early the following day and went to the restaurant as usual. He spent the entire day in the kitchen, preparing food and tasting new recipes. However, his mind was elsewhere. He couldn't stop thinking about his daughter and how much he missed her. He also couldn't stop thinking about Smrithi and her words.

As he was leaving the restaurant, he noticed a poster of a culinary festival in Hyderabad. He booked two tickets and a flight for the next day without thinking twice. Their daughter was looking forward to the festival. The last time she walked out of the restaurant, she looked at the poster and told him, “Nana, I would love to go there and just inhale the aromas of different regions of India and feel the emotions of people via the cuisine.”

In Hyderabad, Sethu and Smrithi visited several restaurants, met with chefs, and attended cooking workshops. They even met a few old friends, but none of them could shake off the feeling of sadness that followed them everywhere they went.

One day, as they were walking down the streets of Hyderabad, they stumbled upon a small restaurant, and something about it caught their attention. They walked in and sat down, and as Smrithi looked through the menu, she noticed their daughter’s favourite dish. Her heart sank.

The waiter approached him and asked, “What can I get you, sir?”

“I’ll have the Usirikaya Pachadi with a side of rice, please,” Smrithi said, pointing to the dish on the menu. Sethu was surprised and he looked up; this was like a café in a tropical land. It mainly had dishes from around the world, and Usirikaya Pachadi (gooseberry pickle) could not be on the menu.

The waiter smiled. “Excellent choice, Sir. That’s one of our most popular dishes.”

As both of them waited for the food, Sethu noticed a man sitting at a nearby table, staring at him. "Is there something I can help you with?" Sethu asked.

The man stood up and walked over to his table. "I couldn't help but notice your accent," said the stranger.

Sethu nodded. "Yes, I was born there but moved to India after I got married; I am an American citizen who loves India and divides time between New York and Bangalore."

"I'm also from America. My name is John. Do you mind if I join you?"

Sethu shrugged. "Sure, why not?"

As they started talking, Sethu learned that John was also a chef and the owner of the café they were in. They talked about food and recipes, and even shared a few cooking tips.

After their meal, John invited Sethu and Smrithi to see his kitchen. As they walked, John asked them, "So, what brings you to Hyderabad?"

Smirthi hesitated momentarily, unsure if they should share their personal story. But something about John made them comfortable, and Sethu said something that he never expected he would to a stranger: "We lost our daughter a few months ago, and we are here to clear our mind, do things that she would have wanted us to do, and hopefully find the courage to cook her favourite dish."

Talking to a stranger about their grief was surprisingly calming; he did not question them about how she passed away. He did not try to give them hope but opened up their feelings.

John nodded sympathetically. "I'm sorry for your loss. But it's good that you're here. Sometimes, a change of scenery can do wonders for the soul," he said. They spoke about their lives and ate heartily. Both of them laughed with their whole hearts for the first time.

"I would love it if you could join my family for dinner tonight," said John. Initially, Sethu and Smriti hesitated to accept the invitation. However, John sensed their apprehension and asked, "What would your daughter do?" And lo and behold, they arrived at John's home right around the corner from the café. John introduced them to his family, and they spent the rest of the evening cooking together.

Smrithi and Sethu were surprised to find Usirikaya Murabba in the white box beside them when they set the dinner table. It triggered a memory for them both. Smrithi looked at John and asked, "John, I've been meaning to ask you this: you have Usirikaya Pachadi as a part of your menu, and now we see this Murabba, both of which are surprisingly similar to the ones my mother used to make with our daughter and a dish that is quite famous in Sethu's restaurant. I don't understand your unusual love for this fruit," she wondered.

John smiled at her and said, "That is one long story, but let me make it short for you.

I was born to an American father and an Indian mother. My mother flew from Suryapet to America to pursue her dreams. She adapted slowly to the American lifestyle, people, places, and culture. When

I was born, she and my Nana travelled to India to meet her parents; it was difficult during those days to make a yearly journey, so they saved up and brought me to India when I was five. My Americanness, if I may call it, could not take Indian food. Everything was put to the test. My parents filled a large suitcase with canned baby food, milk powder, etc., which lasted only a short time.

So both my grandmothers decided to take matters into their own hands. You have to know that in those days, everything was seasonal. So they decided to give me a tiny taste of the seasonal fruits and vegetables, and if I ever liked them, they would cook them for me. Surprisingly, I fell in love with Usirikaya.

My Bamma and Ammama[4] decided to make Usikaraya Murabba, Usirikaya Pachadi, Usirikaya Annam, and whatnot. What happened after that was magic; my stomach felt like someone was singing a soothing lullaby. That is how Usiri came into my life, via the love of two women who took it upon themselves to cook up a storm for their grandchild."

Sethu's eyes lit up. He said, "Oh, John, you would not believe it if I told you our daughter grew up in Usirikaya. She is the one who insisted that we have an entire section in the menu dedicated to only seasonal veggies and fruits."

Over the past year, Smrithi has never seen Sethu's eyes light up like this.

---

4 Ammama - Maternal Grandmother

"Oh, and wait till you hear something even crazier. A few years ago, a young woman walked into our café; she must have been 20. She said she was here with her ammama and wanted to know if we serve anything Indian, and one of my chefs was in for a thorough scolding from the ammama. I believe it was nighttime, and he proudly told them that they had Usirikaya and rice, and lo and behold, the ammama was so upset." So, my chef called me, and I came running; she looked at me and asked me, "Neeku telidu Usirikaya ratri thinukoNanu ani (don't you know that gooseberry pickle should not be had at night)?" I apologised and told her that I did know.

She told me, "Usirikaya is excessively acidic and known to contain high levels of pure and abundant vitamin C. If amla is eaten at night, the acidity rises, which might cause heartburn. Amla also promotes increased energy flow, which could lead to sleep disturbances. As the blood flow quickens, activity levels may rise, which causes insomnia. For this reason, amla should not be consumed at night. She also left me with an idiom, wait, let me remember it."

Smrithi completed his sentence, "Karathalamalakamu," and John said, "That is how easy this should be for you, **just like a gooseberry fits into your palm!**"

Sethu was looking through his phone albums and found a photo of their daughter with her amamma in front of a café; that was where they were that day. He showed that photo to John and Smrithi. For a few minutes, there was silence. Everyone around the table knew they had to say nothing. Sethu and Smrithi returned to their hotel the next day, feeling more rejuvenated than they had in months. They spent the rest of the trip exploring the city, trying new foods, and meeting new people.

When they returned home, both felt like their daughter was back in the house, smiling widely and asking them to move on with life. Sethu went to the kitchen and started cooking his daughter's favourite dish. It was a simple meal, but he ensured every ingredient was perfect, just as she liked it. When he finished, he placed the dish in front of his wife, and they both looked at it for a moment, tears welling up in their eyes.

"It's perfect," Smrithi said, her voice barely above a whisper.

Sethu smiled, feeling the satisfaction he hadn't felt in months. "I know. She would have loved it."

From that day on, Sethu made the dish every week, which soon became a tradition in their home. He even added his own twists to the recipe, experimenting with new flavours and ingredients.

And every time he cooked, he felt as if his daughter was right there with him, enjoying the food and reminding him that even though she was gone, her memory would always live on.

It wasn't easy, but with the help of new friends and a change of scenery, Sethu and Smrithi could heal and find the strength to pay tribute to their daughter in the best way they knew, by cooking her favourite dish with love and care.

Although Smrithi knew that she and Sethu would never fully recover from the loss of their daughter, they both found solace in the kitchen and writing a cookbook dedicated to their daughter; the book had a recipe for every turn in life, and this is where they could keep her memory alive and honour her legacy in the best way they could. Turning the sourness of Usirikaya into something that keeps us healthy and happy is what their daughter taught them.

Here's a recipe for Usirikaya Murabba: A small bedtime story that ammamma would tell the granddaughter. "Usiri is known as one of the foods high in vitamin C and has been part of the Indian diet since time immemorial. While meditating intensely on Lord Vishnu, Lord Brahma had tears rolling down his eyes. When these tears fell on the ground, the Usiri tree was born. Making Usirikaya murabba from these small, tart fruits is one of the best ways to enjoy it. You get all the benefits of amla sweetly. And, my darling, you and I love it too."

Usirikaya Candy Recipe (Gooseberry Sweet Preserves)

Ingredients

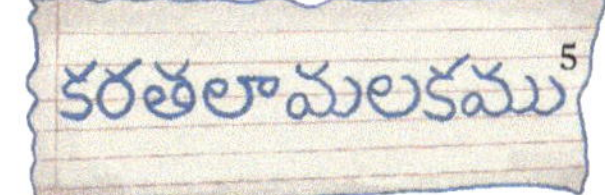

- 500 g Usirikaya (Indian gooseberries)
- 250 g sugar
- 1/2 teaspoon black salt
- 2 tablespoons lemon juice

Instructions

1. **Prepare the Usirikaya:**
    - Wash the Usirikaya thoroughly to remove any dirt or impurities.
    - Freeze the cleaned Usirikaya overnight. Freezing softens the fruit and makes it easier to handle.
    - The next day, allow the frozen Usirikaya to thaw at room temperature. Once thawed, the fruit will easily break into four pieces when gently pressed or cut.
2. **Cook the Usirikaya:**
    - Place a thick-bottomed pot on medium heat and add the thawed Usirikaya pieces.

5 కరతలామలకము (Karathalamalakamu) - as easy as fitting a gooseberry in the palm of your hand

- Add the sugar to the pot and stir continuously. As the sugar dissolves, it will mix with the natural juices of the Usirikaya, creating a syrupy consistency.
- Continue stirring to ensure the sugar doesn't stick to the bottom of the pot. This process takes about 5 minutes.

3. **Monitor the Texture:**

   - As the Usirikaya cooks, it will begin to soften and take on a light brown hue.
   - Check the softness by mashing one piece between your fingers; it should be tender and easy to press.

4. **Add Flavour:**

   - Once the Usirikaya is soft, sprinkle in 1/2 teaspoon of black salt. The salt balances the sweetness and enhances the overall flavour of the dish.
   - Stir well to incorporate the salt evenly.
   - Add 2 tablespoons of freshly squeezed lemon juice to the mixture and stir again. The lemon juice adds a tangy note and acts as a natural preservative.

5. **Cool and Store:**

   - Turn off the heat and allow the mixture to cool completely in the pot.
   - Once cooled, transfer the Usirikaya candy into a clean, dry, airtight container.

- ○ Store the container in a cool, dry place. The candy will keep well for up to six months if stored properly.

6. **Serving Suggestion:**
   - ○ Enjoy one piece of Usirikaya candy after lunch. Its unique sweet, tangy, and slightly salty flavour makes it a delightful digestive treat.

Tips

- Use a thick-bottomed pot to prevent burning and ensure even cooking.
- Adjust the sugar quantity based on your preferred sweetness level.
- Ensure the container is completely dry before storing to prevent spoilage.

This traditional Usirikaya candy is not just a treat but also a natural source of vitamin C and antioxidants, making it a wholesome addition to your post-meal routine.

Salty / Uppaga

My paternal grandfather came to Secunderabad with 25 annas in his pocket, a story he would often tell the whole family, a legend. This story is my tribute to my family, city, and Thatha.

Sprinkled with Love

Going to an Irani café and ordering a "one-by-two" chai with some biscuits was a ritual my grandfather, whom I affectionately called Thatha, had started. He once narrated the story behind this tradition: "I came to Secunderabad with just 25 annas in my pocket and walked into Alpha Café. A man there asked if I could buy him some chai, so I generously ordered one for himself and myself. Only when I went to pay the bill did I realise the chai and my bun maska together cost 25 annas! The owner, observing this from behind the desk, kindly said it was on the house. Since then, I visited the café every Sunday to reminisce about old times with the owner."

Thatha eagerly awaited Sunday, and this time was exclusively ours. We never invited my Nana to join us. Thatha asked him, and my Nana replied, "I'd rather spend my Sunday sleeping than sitting and drinking chai at this place." That was it. Ever since, even if my Nana tried to join, Thatha would say, "No, please go sleep."

Here's my challenge: Thatha passed away 20 days ago and left me a letter with three wishes he wanted me to fulfil for his soul to attain peace, or Moksham. I don't believe in all that, but I must do this for him. Thatha was and is my role model.

Wish number one: I must visit the café daily until we finish his final rituals.

Wish number two: I must order Osmania Biscuits and eat one daily. I don't just eat but try to write down the ingredients in the biscuit!

Wish number three: I need to serve everyone the biscuits for Thatha's final rituals, then take a few to the café and leave them on a plate to see if anyone can tell the difference between the café-made ones and mine.

Knowing my Thatha, he had a reason behind asking me to do this. When I told my parents, my father broke down. He said, "It was our childhood ritual. He was posted at the Secunderabad station when I was seven years old. Until then, Nana had to keep travelling constantly. Every evening, he would finish his work, go to the café, pack hot onion samosas and Osmania Biscuits, and come home. We would sit under the amla tree, sip tea, and have these biscuits and samosas. I would tell him about my day at school, and he would treat me like a mature person and tell me about his day. Later, your grandmother would join us. Then we had your uncles and aunts. He tried his best to spend time with me, but his work and this large family took up his time, and I grew distant. He did try bringing those memories back when you were 7, and I just refused to join you and him for that chai!"

Now I knew why Thatha wanted me to do this; he knew Nana couldn't, as he would be completely immersed in the rituals which Thatha believed in. However, he wanted us to continue this ritual at home by sitting together, sipping chai, and spending a few hours together as a family.

And here's how the next ten days went:

Day 1: It was chaotic; everyone wanted me to be at home. However, I needed to get that recipe right. So I walked into the café and ate at least ten biscuits to guess the ingredients. Let's just say I wouldn't eat those biscuits for six months!

Day 2: Back at the café, the waiter smiled at me and asked, "Nanaaji[6] nahi dikhrey?" *(where's your Grandpa?)* I told him about Thatha, and they all came to pay their condolences and asked for my home address. These folks had known Thatha for many years, yet they didn't know where he lived. I love these café friendships, where strangers become your support, listen to everything you say, talk about every topic in a café, and then part ways to face the real world.

Day 3: I went to the café, and finally, this time, I took a book and a pen. But now I had to eat the biscuits again. I used to love munching on them, but now, I dreaded having one more. But Thatha left me with no choice. So I bit in, and the first taste I tasted was of milk powder; then I took a guess and wrote down maida.

Day 4: Back to the café, and this time, everyone knew what my deal was with the biscuits. So when I sat down, a plate of biscuits and chai was sent to my table, and Thatha's friends at the café sat down to discuss the biscuits. Ramji Thatha said, "Remember, Ramesh, when Suri wanted to buy the whole jar of biscuits?" They all started to laugh. "Share the joke with me, too," I said. So

6 Nanaaji - a way of addressing Grandfather in Hindi

Ramji Thatha noted, "Once, we planned to go to another café to try chai. However, the owner here learned about our plans and was adamant that he would not serve us chai and biscuits. So, your Thatha went to the counter and told him, *Maaf karna (Apologies), but I shall buy your whole jar of biscuits to make up to you.* The owner refused outright, and every day, we would come to sit here and chat, but with no chai. It took us a week to finally join the circle back!"

Day 5: I went to the café, and the server gave me a book. He said, "Sir, woh Reshma Aapa ne diya aapke liye, is mein unke khandani biscuit ka recipe hai." *(Sir, Reshma Aapa left this for you; It has her family's biscuit recipe.)* I asked him, "Who is Reshma Aapa?" He pointed me towards the road, and I could see a lady walking away from the café. I started walking towards her, but she sat in a car and drove away. Disappointed, I returned home.

Day 6: Today, I wanted to avoid going to the café; I wondered who this Reshma Aapa was and why she gave me the recipe. It was an old notebook that must have been opened and closed more than 1,000 times. The pages were yellow, and there was a scent of spices, and a few pages had turmeric and other masalas spread in the corners, perhaps as an ode to some memory. I spent the day reading this notebook at the café.

Notebook Page 1: "Reshma, Arif loved your cooking. He told me how much he enjoyed watching you cook and how you taught him to cook and broke all the stereotypes at home. He said it felt like watching a monk meditating.

I know you stopped cooking after he passed away. However, I'd like you to know that you can keep your memories alive by keeping notes of them and writing down those recipes for future generations. Keep doing what you love the most; we all know you are hiding a brilliant chef inside you. Tera Bhai, Suri." *(Your Brother)*

Wait, what? What is this? This book is a gift from my Thatha to Aapa. My mind was already down the drain with Thatha's passing away, and this mystery was too much. However, I've decided to put the puzzle back together later; I just want to take the recipe and bake some biscuits.

Day 7: Today was a little heavy; Thatha's elder sister travelled to see her brother from her village. She is five years older than him and does not remember anything. She insisted on seeing him; she wanted to know why he was not talking to her. We did not have the heart to break the news to her. However, she did notice that his photo had a garland, and everyone was crying. But then, she announced loudly, "My brother is alive and happy; why are you crying? Stop this now." It reminded us that though we were sad to have him go away physically, he lived life to the fullest and loved every moment. So, we started talking about his childhood and anecdotes from his life, while his elder sister shared many memories of him.

Oh, I did go to the café. However, I did not have to eat those dreaded biscuits; I do not like them anymore. I am just tired of eating them every day! I asked people who Arif Bhai was, and they told me he owned his café, the one who started the café, promoting his wife's culinary skills.

Day 8: I went to the café and asked my Thatha's friends to take me to Reshma Aapa's home. They came along, and we discovered that Aapa no longer lived there but was away in a nursing home. We drove to the nursing home and Aapa's reaction unfolded in layers, first surprise, then anger, and finally, she broke down into tears upon seeing all of us. She told me that, a few months before Thatha's demise, her family moved her here. And she did not want anyone to find out about it; she was embarrassed. Thatha's friends cried with her and told me how a few of their kids wanted to do this. I was numb and I could not think of anything better to say, so I asked Aapa, "Will you please teach me how to make the biscuits?"

Day 9: Yesterday, I got Aapa home, and she slept in Thatha's room with his sister. In the morning, both Aapa and Paati[7] behaved like long-lost sisters. I forced Paati to take a break and got Aapa to the kitchen. And here is how it went. "Sethu, for the biscuits to turn out tasty, we first need patience and pure ingredients," said Aapa. "I usually take homemade butter, but if you cannot get that, get butter from your local milk vendor or buy a trusted brand. A tip: Don't leave the butter in the fridge. Keep it in a box or a tiffin box and leave it outside at room temperature. If the butter is in the fridge or not soft enough to spread on the bread, pour hot water into a ceramic or glass cup or bowl, something inside which you can keep your butter. After a few minutes, drain the

7 Paati - Grandmother

water out of the vessel and quickly cover your butter. The heat from the cup/bowl will soften your butter in just a few minutes."

I stood there watching Aapa make the first batch, and then I dived in to make the second batch. The first few attempts were futile. My biscuits were breaking or soft as chewy gum. However, after multiple attempts, I finally got five perfect biscuits late in the evening.

Day 10: Today, they say Thatha's soul bids goodbye to the mortal world and starts moving towards the light. We cook dishes that have been Thatha's favourite and serve them to everyone. I know my five biscuits would not be enough for more than 300 families, friends, and strangers who Thatha had helped, like many others, without ever announcing it to the world. And also the ten dogs that Thatha took care of in our lane. As we were thinking about what to do, we saw the present owner of the café, along with the staff, walking in carrying tins of Osmania Biscuits.

He said, "Thatha, through you, showed me how a person's simple act of learning something without asking for anything brings joy to them and all of us. I have been watching you since you walked into that café, eager to learn how to make biscuits. And the whole restaurant has been betting on this recipe. At first, I was angry that you did not come to me for the recipe. But then, when I saw Aapa, I realised it was never mine from the beginning; it belonged to everyone. I must thank your Thatha for teaching us this act of being humble even when he is not around us."

Everyone who came was surprised to find biscuits on the menu! I was too happy to eat and forgot to taste the biscuits. The next day, a quiet Sunday, I suddenly heard my Thatha's scooter roar to life. Curious and surprised, I rushed outside to see who had started it only to find it was my Nana. "Let's get some chai and Osmania Biscuits at the café!" he said.

Oh, and we did place a plate of biscuits on the table at the café for everyone to try.

Osmania Biscuits Recipe

Ingredients

- 200g unsalted butter
- 260 g all-purpose flour (maida)
- 3 teaspoons powdered milk
- 1 teaspoon salt
- 100 g powdered sugar
- 2 teaspoons baking powder
- Milk (for brushing before baking)

Instructions

1. **Preparation:**
   - Line two baking pans with parchment paper and set them aside.
   - Preheat your oven to 200°C (392°F).
2. **Mix the Dry Ingredients:**
   - Sift together the all-purpose flour, baking powder and salt in a mixing bowl. Set aside.

3. **Cream the Butter:**
    - In a separate large bowl, add the unsalted butter. Cream the butter with a rubber or silicone spatula until it becomes soft and smooth. This step ensures the biscuits have a tender texture.
4. **Combine Butter and Dry Ingredients:**
    - Gradually add the sifted flour mixture to the creamed butter in small portions. Mix gently after each addition to avoid forming lumps.
    - Once all the flour is incorporated, gently knead or massage the dough with your hands. Be careful not to overwork the dough; use light motions to incorporate air, giving the biscuits their lightness.
    - The dough should feel light and turn slightly whitish as you knead.
5. **Add the Remaining Ingredients:**
    - Add the powdered sugar, powdered milk, and a pinch of soy flour (optional for additional texture). Knead the mixture thoroughly to combine, ensuring the dough becomes smooth and uniform.
    - If the dough feels sticky, refrigerate it for 10–15 minutes to make it easier to handle.
6. **Roll and Shape the Biscuits:**
    - Divide the dough into two equal portions.
    - On a lightly floured work surface, roll out one portion of the dough to a thickness of about 1/4 inch.

- Use a 3-inch round cookie cutter to cut out biscuit shapes. Transfer the cut biscuits to the prepared baking sheet.
- Repeat with the remaining dough.

7. **Brush with Milk:**

    - Brush the tops of the biscuits lightly with room-temperature milk. This step helps achieve a golden-brown finish during baking.

8. **Bake the Biscuits:**

    - Place the baking trays in the oven and bake for 20–25 minutes, or until the biscuits turn a light golden brown. Keep an eye on them in the last few minutes to prevent overbaking.

9. **Cool and Store:**

    - Remove the biscuits from the oven and transfer them to a wire rack to cool completely.
    - Once cooled, store the biscuits in an airtight container. They will stay fresh for up to two weeks (or longer in cooler weather).

Tips

- Use high-quality butter for the best flavour, as it forms the recipe's base.

- Refrigerating the dough helps firm it up, making it easier to roll and cut into shapes.
- If you prefer slightly softer biscuits, reduce the baking time, keeping a close watch.

These Osmania Biscuits are perfect with a cup of chai or coffee, offering a rich, buttery texture with a touch of sweetness. A timeless treat that can be enjoyed at any time!

Bitter / Cheedu

I've seen and experienced life when communication becomes a silent spectator. This story is my perception of that.

Bitter Roots, Healing Hearts

Meetu was a teenage girl living in a busy city. She always had the quality of being kind to other people. Meetu used to giggle and tell her parents, "I think I am kind like Thatha, and I like being compared to him," when they argued that she had gone on one of them for being nice.

Meetu had a hectic schedule. She would go to school, come home, rest, and then go to her silambam (an old Indian martial art from Tamilnadu) lessons twice a week and her dancing class three days a week. She had the keys to the house; both of her parents were employed, and she spent the hours after classes by herself. Her parents trusted her and allowed her to be independent, even though they had just recently relocated to a new colony. By 5:00 p.m., both of her parents returned home.

Additionally, CCTV cameras were installed, and Meetu rode the same bus to and from school. Although she missed her old colony pals, she was somewhat at ease because Radhika, her schoolmate, was from the same colony. Occasionally, she visited Radhika's home and Radhika visited hers.

Radhika felt comfortable and free at Meetu's house. There was an air of strict discipline in Radhika's house. They could not talk or do whatever they liked. Radhika's parents were like tiger parents. They would frequently enquire about Meetu's grades and favourite subjects. They would say, "Talk about courses or read about this subject or that," when she and Radhika were talking about movies or their favourite actors. It was like they were not allowed to have any conversations other than studies, or grades. Gradually, Meetu stopped going to Radhika's house.

Meetu's bicycle tyre punctured one day as she was riding back from her dance lesson. She took it to the closest shop to fix it. As she waited, she conversed with another girl who introduced herself and said she lived in a nearby colony. "I moved here a few months ago with my parents, and I get bored because there is no one I know," the girl, Amala, told her. I started riding my bike outside to see if I could make new friends. I didn't meet anyone for several weeks, but I recently met a girl named Radhika.

Meetu raised her ears. "Radhika!" she added, "I know her; she lives two rows from my house." "I apologise, but where are my manners?" Meetu enquired. "Meetu is my name; and you are?" she asked. "I am so happy to know two people from all over the world! My name is Amala," Amala said. They both burst out laughing.

As her cycle was fixed, Meetu replied, "I have to leave now." But let's get together tomorrow at the same time and location, and I'll give Radhika a call as well.

"Oh, that would be amazing," Amala remarked.

Meetu, Radhika, and Amala soon became a trio. Amala enrolled in the same classes as Meetu, and they would spend hours conversing at Meetu's house. Since her parents believed that extracurricular activities impacted her academic performance, Radhika could not attend those classes. Instead, she had to attend a variety of tuition classes to complete her 12th grade with A+ marks.

Everything went smoothly for the first couple of years, and Meetu's parents were pleased to watch Meetu and Amala's friendship blossom. Amala's mother had visited Meetu's house a few weeks ago to introduce herself, so they didn't worry that they had never met Amala's parents. Meetu's mother, who liked clothing and was always proud of her impeccable taste in house linens, was overjoyed that Amala's mother was operating her own linens company. Amala's mother suggested they go to their factory so Meetu's mother could select the materials she wanted for the upholstery and have them printed with special designs.

One day, Meetu's parents got a call from the school, asking them to see the principal immediately.

"Is everything okay at home?" the principal inquired.

"Yes, everything is good at home," Vara and Ravi responded, exchanging glances. "Please tell us why you called us today. Is Meetu doing well? Can we speak with her? Is she unwell? Would you mind if we went to her class, or could you call her here?" they asked.

"Meetu has not been coming to school for the past few days, and her attendance has been erratic," the principal added after giving them a worried look. She has been signing your names on the letter. I called you because the class teacher was unsure whether the letters were authentic.

Neither parent knew how to respond or what to say.

"Is she present at school today?" Vara inquired. The principal gave a resounding no.

Meetu's parents hurried out and drove directly home before the principal could say anything.

The front door was locked. They both searched the colony for her. Meetu called them just as they were about to leave for the police station. "Amma, Nana." She was still wearing her school uniform and riding her cycle. Meetu was going to hear something nasty from Mrs. Vara. However, squeezing her hand fiercely, Ravi held her back.

"I thought you were at school, Meetu," Ravi stated. "Yes, Nana, I did attend school, but after getting permission from the principal, I came home due to a severe stomach ache."

Later in the evening, Mrs. Vara suggested that they should eat dinner on the terrace, sitting under the moonlight and unwinding. Meetu declined, stating that she needed to relax because she was still experiencing stomach pain.

"Why are you complaining of a stomach ache when you were having a good time riding your bike around the colony in the afternoon?" Vara was asked. "Stop lying to us; your principal and we know you have been skipping school." After saying this, she entered Meetu's room and began searching for items that could provide insight into her recent actions.

She discarded every poster and item that Meetu had painstakingly collected over the years. After hearing the commotion, Ravi entered the room. He saw Vara searching through all the drawers and flinging everything on the floor, papers and trinkets crammed in every corner. He moved ahead and tightly embraced Vara. He said, “Shhh, shhh, it’s okay, it’s okay, let it all go, the sadness, the anger, let it all go.”

Vara turned around and began to cry, saying, “I don’t know what’s going on with our daughter.” “Look, Meetu, I’m sorry,” she murmured, turning to discover that Meetu had vanished from the room. It was eight o’clock at night. When they both left the room, they saw the front door open. They thought Meetu went out in the rain and called for her, “Meetu, Meetu.” But there was no answer from her.

Vara hurried inside and dialled a number. “Hello, this is a surprise,” said Radhika’s mother. “You could have just walked by.” “Is Meetu at your place?” Mrs. Vara asked. “No, she isn’t. Is everything okay?” Radhika’s mother responded, but Vara abruptly ended the call before she could finish her sentence.

An identical response came when she dialled Amala’s number next.

As she raced outside, she noticed Ravi getting his bike going. “Come, let’s search for her in the colony,” he urged. Meetu was seated on the patio, screaming and wailing during all of this.

After an hour, both parents returned home. “Should we call the police?” Mr. Vara inquired. “Let’s wait until tomorrow morning,” Vara said. They noticed Meetu walking down the stairs as they entered the house. She walked past them, entered her room, and shut the door. The parents were unaware of what was happening because this was all new to them. But they fell asleep once they both settled into the recliners across from her room.

Ravi got up and made himself and his wife a cup of coffee. He gently nudged Vara to get up, waited for her to finish freshening up and said, “Let’s think from a calm mind; she has never behaved this way and was always a daughter that others took inspiration from; for the first time, she lied to us and is not ready to talk to us. I understand that you and I are both upset, so let’s have a conversation and find out what is bothering her. However, we both saw what happened yesterday when we got angry.” He then went to knock on Meetu’s door.

Even before he could knock on the door, Meetu opened the door, looked at him, hugged him, and started sobbing. Vara came running from the place where she was sitting and said, “I am sorry, my baby, I am terribly sorry for my behaviour yesterday. You see, I was never taught to be a mother; I am learning every day and what happened yesterday was new. I am sorry for behaving like that, I am so sorry.” All three of them hugged each other. They all decided to skip school and the office and just stay home.

They decided to put on their favourite movie. Ravi got lunch from their favourite Dhaba. While they were watching the movie, Ravi nudged Vara to start the conversation with Meetu. Meetu refused to talk to them. The minute they started the conversation, she said she was tired and went straight to her room.

Slowly, they started noticing changes in Meetu; she was not the same girl they knew. She refused to meet her friends, was always huddled up in the room and only went out once for a walk in the evening.

"Ravi, I am not sure what to do. We have tried everything we could, and she still refuses to tell us what is bothering her. Seeing her like this is making you and me sad," Vara said.

The root of Meetu's bitterness and sadness was a secret buried deep within her heart, a secret she feared would hurt her parents more than it pained her.

After numerous attempts to understand her behaviour, they sent her to her maternal grandparents' house in a quaint village, hoping the change of scenery would help her find solace.

The village was a world away from the city's chaos, where nature's tranquillity reigned supreme. Meetu's grandparents warmly welcomed her, but she remained distant, guarding her secret closely.

Every morning, Meetu would accompany her grandfather to the fields, only to find solace atop a neem tree, gazing into the horizon. Her grandfather, a man of few words, respected her silence, knowing that some wounds needed healing time.

One day, he approached her with an idea. "Meetu," he began, "how about we try something different today? I'll teach you a special recipe. It's a dish that's bitter to taste but has healing properties. Like this dish, understanding and confronting our bitterness can lead to healing."

Intrigued by the analogy, Meetu agreed. As they prepared the dish together, her grandfather prodded, "You know, Meetu, it's okay to share your burdens. Sometimes, our weight becomes lighter when we open up to someone."

Meetu hesitated, then finally whispered, "Grandpa, I'm scared. I'm scared that if I tell my parents the truth, it will hurt them more than it hurts me."

Her grandfather put down the spoon and looked at her with kind eyes. "My child, your parents' love for you is stronger than any pain. They would want to share your burden, not be shielded from it. Keeping this secret is like allowing a wound to fester. It needs air and light to heal."

Tears welled up in Meetu's eyes as she slowly opened up about the abuse she had faced, a secret she had kept hidden for so long.

Thatha said, Meetu, "I met a friend in my colony. Her name is Amala, and she is a great friend who is always ready to help me. Radhika, Amala, and I have become very close; you remember Radhika, don't you? You met her when you came to the city last time."

Her grandfather Satyanarayana said, "Oh yes, I remember her, isn't she the one who loves our house as nobody asks both of you to study," he said, laughing. This broke the tension and Meetu also laughed.

Meetu came closer to her Thatha and started, "The first time I went to Amala's house, I was taken aback at how huge her home was; she and her brother have vast rooms of their own. I would go into each room and pretend like I was the queen of a castle. One day, while I was in the room, a man came in and even before I could say something, he tightly..." Meetu started panting and sweating... and sobbing.

"Meetu, it's okay if you don't tell me everything that happened. Let's go home," said her grandfather. But Meetu wanted her grandfather to know everything.

Her grandfather listened with a heavy heart, offering her the comfort and understanding she desperately needed.

Over the following days, Meetu's grandparents became her pillars of strength. They encouraged her to face her fears and assured her that her parents' love would not waver in the face of this revelation.

With newfound courage, Meetu decided to return home and share her truth. Her grandparents accompanied her back to the city, providing her with the support she needed during this difficult time. Her parents, shocked and heartbroken by her ordeal, enveloped her in their love and support. They apologised for not seeing her pain earlier and promised to stand beside her as she healed.

Understanding the importance of believing Meetu and taking the matter seriously, her parents spoke to the concerned authorities and ensured that action was taken. The once bitter relationship between Meetu and her parents transformed into mutual understanding and unwavering support.

The village, the neem tree, and the bitter dish remained etched in Meetu's memory, symbols of her journey from darkness to light. Meetu learned that sharing her pain was not a sign of weakness but a step towards healing. And in her parents' unwavering love, she found her greatest strength.

udaan
मैंने
प्यार किया
SHIV

Neem-Guava Chutney Recipe

Ingredients

- A handful of fresh neem leaves.
- A handful of fresh guava leaves.
- 1 teaspoon jeera (cumin) powder
- Salt, to taste
- 1 small piece of ginger
- 1 green chilli (adjust to taste)
- 1/2 teaspoon red chilli powder
- 1/4 teaspoon asafoetida (hing)
- 1 teaspoon ghee

Instructions

1. **Boil the Ingredients:**
    - Add the neem leaves, guava leaves, ginger, green chilli, cumin powder, red chilli powder, and salt to a water-filled vessel.
    - Bring the mixture to a boil and let it simmer for about 3 minutes.
2. **Prepare the Paste:**
    - Once boiled, strain the mixture and discard the water.
    - Transfer the boiled ingredients to a grinder and blend them into a smooth paste.

3. **Tempering the Chutney:**
    - Heat a pan on medium heat and add ghee.
    - Once the ghee melts, add asafoetida (hing) and sauté for about 30 seconds to release its aroma.
    - Add the prepared chutney paste to the pan and mix well.
    - Fry the chutney on low heat for about 2 minutes, stirring constantly to ensure it doesn't stick to the pan.

4. **Serve:**
    - Remove the chutney from the heat and let it cool slightly.
    - Serve as a side dish with rice, dosa, or chapati, or use it as a flavourful spread.

Tips:

- Adjust the green and red chilli levels based on your spice tolerance.
- To add depth of flavour, lightly toast the cumin powder before adding it.
- Store any leftover chutney in an airtight container in the refrigerator for up to 2 days.

This **Neem-Guava Chutney** is a unique blend of flavours with a hint of bitterness from the neem, balanced by the earthiness of guava leaves and spices. Neem-guava chutney is perfect for adding a touch of health and tradition to your meal!

Pungent / Ghatu

My Nana was my guru when it came to food, culture, and history; he was a walking encyclopedia. His teaching style was efficient and filled with laughter and joy. This is my homage to him.

A Taste of Past

Our kitchen at home, with its cold red oxide floor beneath my bare feet, was a haven of memories. The earthy perfume of the rain-soaked banana leaves swinging just outside the open window blended with the comforting aroma of spices. Their rustling motions sounded like a song of our ancestry, a tune written by generations before me.

"Nana," I asked quietly, my voice shaking with want. "Is it time? Will you eventually reveal Kanda Bachali's secrets to me?"

He turned with a smile that radiated the warmth of years spent tending farms and nurturing lives, spreading across his worn face. An elephant yam waited on the chopping board, and his hands, worn from decades of work, rested softly on it.

"Maya," he whispered, his voice soft and lulling, like a soothing lullaby. "Yes, the time has come. Like our name and this house, this too is your inheritance. The moment has arrived for you to carry it forward."

I gazed admiringly as he started to peel the yam, his motions methodical and rehearsed. The pale flesh underneath was exposed as the sharp knife sliced through the tight skin.

"You know, Nana," I said, tracing my gaze down his calm hands, "your cooking has a certain magic. You seem to be a magician, casting spells of memory and taste."

His loud, resonant laugh reverberated around the kitchen. "Yes, but without comprehension, magic cannot exist. My love, cooking is about the heart as much as the hands. You'll discover the formula for that magic today."

I felt a deep connection as he handed me the yam as if the weight of that inconspicuous vegetable held the soul of our heritage. I carefully cut and sliced, imitating his motions, my hands shaking slightly then steadying with his encouraging nods.

I was intrigued; I asked, "Nana, did Bamma teach you this? How did you learn it?"

His eyes softened as he got lost in a past I could only speculate about; his knife, resting on the cutting board. "Yes," he answered, with a hint of want. "In the same way that her mother taught her, she taught me. Maya, this dish is more than just food. It's a narrative. She gave it to me, and now I'm giving it to you."

Nana started making the spice mixture while the yam and greens slowly simmered on the stove. He ground a tiny pile of mustard seeds, soaked rice, and flaming red chillies into a fragrant paste in a stone mortar. The repetitive sound of the pestle hitting the stone was as calming as the sounds of a temple drum.

"This," he remarked, displaying the bowl of bright red paste, "is the essence of the mixture. This is where the harmony of tanginess, earthiness, and spice is achieved."

I leaned closer and breathed in the strong, acrid scent. "So, this is the secret to Kanda Bachali Kura?"

"One of many secrets," he winked in response. Let's add the tamarind now. That's where the dish's distinctive sour kick comes from.

We moved in unison as the hours passed, and our movements were silent dances arranged according to custom. A familiar and reassuring symphony was produced by the pot simmering, the sizzling of spices, and Nana's soft voice.

The scent was so strong at one time that my younger brother Arjun stormed into the kitchen. Excitement glistened in his wide eyes as he cried, "Is it done yet? I am so excited!"

Nana turned to face him, the crinkles at the corners of his eyes getting more profound as he laughed. "Be patient, Arjun. There is more to Sankranthi than just the cuisine. It's about family time, prayers, and customs we follow. That's what gives the feast its significance."

At last, the food was prepared. We served it on fresh banana leaves, contrasting nicely with the curry's deep golden colour. The sound of clinking spoons, laughter, and stories filled the kitchen.

I took a piece and exclaimed, "Nana, this meal, it's like stepping into our past. Each flavour, the sharpness of tamarind, the earthy yam, and the powerful mustard paste, tells a tale. It resembles a tapestry made of woven memories."

With a bite, Arjun, ever the jester, said, "All I know is, it's heavenly!"

With pride in his eyes, Nana put a hand on my shoulder. "Remember, Maya, that each dish we prepare represents a part of who we are, our past, love, and hardships. It's a legacy, not simply food. You are now a part of that legacy."

My eyes filled with tears as I hugged him. "I swear, Nana, one meal at a time, I'll continue our tale."

I understood that Kanda Bachali Kura was more than just a dish as we ate dinner together, it was a link to our forefathers, a testament to tenacity, and a celebration of unity. It served as a reminder that even the most essential ingredients have the capacity to unite people across generations.

And with this meal, I invite you into our story, a tale of love, legacy, and the enduring bonds of family, rather than merely sharing a taste of tradition.

1989 jan
ALWY

Kanda Bachali (Elephant Foot Yam and Malabar Spinach Curry)

Ingredients

- 250g elephant foot yam (kanda), peeled and cubed
- 1 stalk of Malabar spinach (bachali kura), chopped
- 2 tbsp peanut oil (or any neutral oil)
- 1 tbsp raw rice (soaked)
- 4 tsp mustard seeds (split)
- 4 dried red chillies (soaked)
- 3 green chillies, slit
- A pinch of asafoetida (hing)
- 1 sprig of curry leaves
- Gooseberry-sized tamarind, soaked in 1/2 cup of warm water
- Salt, as required

Instructions

1. **Prepare the Tamarind Water:**
    - Soak the tamarind in 1/2 cup of warm water for about 10 minutes. Extract the juice and set aside.

2. **Cook the Vegetables:**
    - Peel the elephant foot yam and cut it into medium-sized cubes. Chop the Malabar spinach (bachali kura) into manageable pieces.
    - In a thick-bottomed vessel, add the yam, spinach, and enough water just to cover the vegetables.
    - Cook until both the yam and spinach are soft and tender. Once done, drain any excess water and set the cooked vegetables aside.
3. **Prepare the Mustard Paste:**
    - Soak one tbsp of raw rice, two tsp of mustard seeds, and four dried red chillies in water for 15 minutes.
    - Grind the soaked ingredients into a coarse paste and set it aside.
4. **Mash the Yam:**
    - Lightly mash the cooked yam, leaving some chunks intact for texture.
5. **Temper the Spices:**
    - Heat two tbsp oil in a pan over medium heat.
    - Add the remaining two tsp of mustard seeds and let them crackle.
    - Add a pinch of hing (asafoetida), curry leaves, and slit green chillies. Sauté for about 30 seconds until aromatic.

6. **Combine and Cook:**
   - Add the mashed yam and spinach mixture to the pan. Mix well.
   - Stir in the prepared mustard rice paste and mix thoroughly.
   - Add the tamarind water and salt to taste. Cook on low heat for 2–3 minutes, allowing the flavours to meld.
7. **Serve:**
   - Remove from the heat and serve hot with steamed rice.
   - Top with a dollop of ghee for added flavour and richness.

Tips

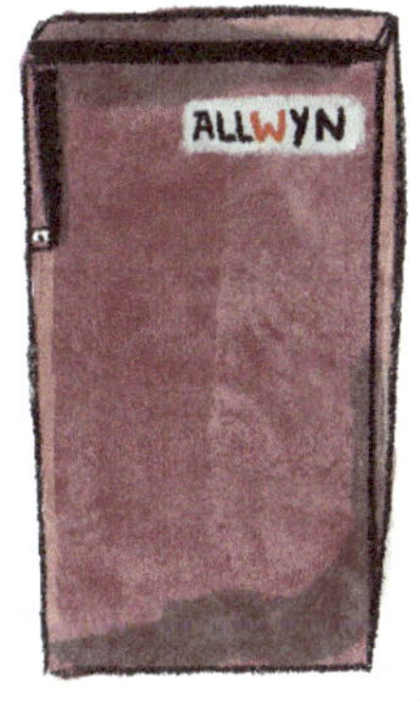

- Ensure the yam is cooked thoroughly to avoid any itchiness in the throat from undercooked pieces.
- Adjust the green and red chillies based on your spice preference.
- For a richer flavour, you can toast the mustard seeds and curry leaves lightly before adding them.

Enjoy this flavourful **Kanda Bachali** with hot rice, a dish that beautifully combines earthy and tangy flavours for a comforting meal.

Spicy / Karam

Summers arrived four months after my mother passed away. In April, she would gather all her goods to make the Avakai Pachadi (the South Indian Telugu mango pickle). I was numb with the feeling of having lost my childhood. Then, I found a tiny book of handmade papers and saw Amma's handwriting. The book contained detailed recipes along with instructions for gardening. I poured my grief into making the Avakai. This story is my connection to food and heritage.

Grief was Spicy

I was at a wedding in Chennai, and Amma was home with the kids. I called her to ask if she needed anything from Chennai. "Amma, what can I get you from Chennai?" I inquired.

"Go to our old house and get those plants we left behind; also, get that large mortar and pestle we left behind," Amma replied.

This was typical of her, never wanting to part with old things, especially plants and her beloved old mortar and pestle. It's been around a year and a few months since she passed away. However, it feels like she is constantly around me, in little things and memories that surface daily.

My mother started cooking more only after my father passed away. Nana loved to cook, and the kitchen was his domain. His love language was food. If Amma did cook, Nana would praise her and playfully comment on the seasoning, winking as he teased her. Their playful banter was a staple in our household, especially during festivals.

Amma aimed to finish the ritual offerings to the gods by noon and wanted the whole family seated for lunch by 1 pm. Nana, however, took his time cooking and savouring the process. "Why are you still on Payasam[8]? Where is the Pulihora[9] for Neivedyam[10]?" Amma would ask Nana.

While praying, Amma repeatedly peeked out to check Nana's progress. He would join her for prayers, but then she'd rush to check on the food. This tug-of-war between fast and slow continued, with Nana usually bringing the food for the offerings at around 1:30 pm, and we'd finish lunch by 3 pm. Despite Amma's frustration, she'd settled into a contented "Bukthaysam" (sleepiness felt after a meal) after a hearty meal and watched a movie on the DD channel, a weekend and festival tradition.

Last year was the first time in 44 years that I did not have my Amma to guide me during these rituals. I was trying to maintain them; her memory was alive in many objects, moments, and rituals. She would get furious if I did not do what she asked me to do, only on these occasions. I used to make fun of it. "What is this, Amma? Just because you want to do something and follow something does not mean I end up partaking in it every single time." She would respond, "I am telling you now, remember these now; once I am gone, you will not only miss me, but these rituals and small things will

8 Payasam - A South-Indian sweet pudding, served as a festival or a Temple dessert.

9 Pulihora - Tamarind-flavoured rice tempered with peanuts, curry leaves, and spices; a common Prasadam (blessed food) in South-Indian temples.

10 Neivedhyam - The temple ritual offering of food to a deity during Hindu worship, presented before it is shared as Prasadam (blessed food).

keep you going." Although her words made me angry, in hindsight, they make sense now.

My mother's life was a never-ending journey of fulfilling duties. She navigated the roles of daughter, sister, wife, mother, and daughter-in-law with unwavering grace and dignity. In our family, she was known as the lioness, one who was fiercely protective of her principles, family, and self-respect.

As a teenager, I saw my mother as my worst enemy. In my mind, she was always holding me back, never letting me forge my own path. Little did I know that one incident would change my entire perspective of her.

I was married into a family vastly different from my own. My ex-husband was insecure, often laughing at me cynically and constantly trying to belittle me. I endured this treatment to keep my parents happy. But one day, I reached my breaking point. My ex-husband threatened to kill me. In a state of panic, I called my mother.

She knew that my patience had worn thin. Whenever she asked me if I wanted to leave, I said, "Let's give him another chance. After all, he's only human." But that day was different.

Within minutes, my mother was at my doorstep. The man who had tormented me ran away at her arrival. She turned to his parents and sister and declared, "I will sit here in your living room until that coward comes home, even if it takes a year. I am not leaving this place with my daughter's head held low. I want to see him, meet him, look him in the eye, and tell him that my daughter has a mother who will kill for her."

The strength I derived from her that day still courses through my veins. My mother, the lioness, showed me the true meaning of protection and dignity.

That summer, I returned home to stay put and filed for divorce. Amma was making pickles. After washing the mangoes, she handed me a considerably large knife exclusively designed to chop the firm raw mangoes into pieces and let me have a ball with that and the mangoes. It felt so liberating; I chopped away all the anger stored in me along with the mangoes.

During the summer pickle-making season, my parents' battle for time management stretched over days. Nana would spend half a day at Monda Market, chatting with vendors to find the best raw mangoes for pickling, while Amma efficiently gathered her ingredients in an hour. Despite her murmurs about Nana's leisurely pace, he'd return with stories of the vendors' lives and their families. Together, they created Avakai, a mango pickle that was the talk of the town. They also crafted many other pickle variants that lasted us the entire year.

I never learned the art of pickle-making from them while they were alive. In 2023, deep in grief after losing my mother and with both my parents and brother gone by the age of 43, I stumbled upon my mother's neatly written Avakai recipe in their diaries. In my 44th year, blending my sorrow with their cherished memory, I made my first batch of mango pickles.

Avakai Pachadi (Mango Pickle) – For Beginners

Ingredients

- 5 cups of mango pieces (preferably from collector mangoes, rasalu, or any firm, unripe mango)
- 1 cup red chilli powder (preferably Three Mangoes brand)
- 1 cup mustard powder (AS brand or homemade)
- 3/4 cup rock salt
- 2 litres of cold-pressed sesame oil (1 litre for mixing, 1 litre for the 3rd day)
- 1/2 cup black channa (optional, washed and dried)
- 1/2 cup of peeled garlic (optional, for the 3rd day)
- 1 tbsp asafoetida (hing)
- 1 tsp methi seeds (fenugreek)

Instructions

1. **Prepare the Mangoes:**
   - Wash the mangoes thoroughly and soak them in water overnight.
   - The next day, wipe the mangoes completely dry using a clean cloth. Ensure no moisture remains, as water can spoil the pickle.
   - Cut the mangoes into medium-sized pieces. Remove the thin layer of the kernel from each piece for better shelf life and flavour.
2. **Mix the Masala:**
   - Mix the red chilli powder, mustard powder, and rock salt in a separate, clean bowl. Add 1 tbsp of asafoetida (hing) and one tsp of methi seeds. Stir the mixture well to combine.
   - Add 1/2 litre of sesame oil to the spice mixture and mix thoroughly to form a paste.
3. **Combine Mangoes and Masala:**
   - Add the mango pieces to a large, clean bowl (preferably steel or ceramic). Gradually coat the mango pieces with the prepared masala paste, ensuring each piece is well covered.
   - Pour in another 1/2 litre of sesame oil and mix well. (If using, you can add the black chana at this stage.)
   - Cover the bowl with a clean plate and set it aside in a cool, dark place. Let the pickle rest for three days without disturbing it.

4. **After Three Days:**
   - On the third day, give the pickle a good stir. You can optionally add 250g of peeled garlic cloves at this stage. Mix the garlic well into the pickle.
   - Top the mixture with more sesame oil, ensuring that thc oil floats abovc thc pickle. This step helps preserve the pickle and enhances its flavour.

5. **Store the Pickle:**
   - Check for salt and adjust if needed, mixing well to incorporate.
   - Transfer the prepared Avakai into a clean, dry ceramic or glass jar. Press it down gently and pour sesame oil on top until the oil forms a protective layer. 
   - Cover the jar with a lid and tie a cotton cloth around the jar's mouth to keep it airtight. Store the jar in a cool, dark place.

6. **Serving and Storage Tips:**
   - Always use a clean, dry spoon to scoop out the pickle. This prevents contamination and extends its shclf life.
   - Transfer small portions into a smaller jar for daily use.
   - The pickle does not need refrigeration and can last for months if stored properly.

Notes for Beginners

- Firm, unripe mangoes are key to achieving the best texture, flavour, and long shelf life.
- Ensure all utensils and jars are completely dry before use to prevent spoilage.
- The oil layer floating on top is a natural preservative, so don't skimp on it.

Enjoy this classic **Avakai Pachadi** with steaming hot rice and a dollop of ghee, a timeless tradition that brings authentic South Indian flavours to your plate.

Acknowledgements

I owe a decade-long friendship to Mounica Tata, who sketched the first portrait for my family a decade ago and later brought this book to life with illustrations. She understands my mind as well as I do. Her art, across these pages, carries the soul of every story.

To my women, you know who you are. You have given me books, shared your lives, and poured your hearts into this project, making it your own. Thank you for keeping me grounded. Your stories have been heard, held, honoured, and engraved in the spirit of these pages.

The books I've read, from Barrister Parvateesam by Mokkapati Narasimha Sastry to my paternal grandmother's handwritten tales about her granddaughters, from Haruki Murakami's Drifting Worlds to Mahasweta Devi's fierce truths, your words have been both my quiet rebellion and my refuge.

To my extended family, thank you for the stories you told me in childhood and the ones I continue to witness in your everyday lives. The legacies of the Chulikuri, Tanikella, and Mouli–Latha families echo through these pages.

To my Matterz family, what would I have done without you? You stood by me in joy, grief, and everyday messy, beautiful chaos. You started as friends, but you became my chosen people somewhere along the way.

To Swaru Pinni, you quietly became my guardian after Amma left, especially when I didn't know I needed one. Your presence held me steady. And to Vindhya, my amazing sister-in-law, our conversations on the terrace about family, legacy, secrets, and grief gifted me a well of memory that I now pour into words.

And to my incredible Instagram family, thank you. I appreciate your kindness and unwavering presence. You reminded me that there is still room for heart in food and stories, and you kept me going when I needed it most.

About the Author

Deepthi Tanikella is a storyteller and food chronicler who finds magic in the everyday moments, especially in kitchens where memories simmer, and traditions come alive. After a rich journey through film, theatre, and corporate life, she turned to food to navigate grief and rediscover joy, honouring the legacy of her late parents and brother through recipes, rituals, and the warmth of shared meals.

She founded Pinch of South, a creative platform where food, culture, and storytelling meet. With a deep love for the history of South Indian food, voices of women's banter in kitchens, and the emotional landscapes of home, Deepthi's work blurs the line between the personal and the collective.

She lives in Bangalore with her husband, four children, and two beloved dogs. A natural host, she thrives on bringing people together, one meal, one story, and one soulful conversation at a time.

You can reach her at deethicooks@gmail.com

About the Illustrator

Mounica Tata is a self taught illustrator, a storytcllcr, an art educator, and an entrepreneur. She married the two loves of her life; art and stories and thus her brand, Doodleodrama was born. She donned multiple hats - assistant editor, copy writer, account manager, and creative lead before quitting everything to tell stories full time through her art in 2016. She's since managed to build a robust community online through her work, dabbled in digital, editorial, and package design. She's worked with multiple brands like Intel, RedBull, Amazon Prime, One Plus, Netflix. And worked with organisations such as ITC, World Vision, Simply Sports.

Mounica lives in Bengaluru with her husband and their two adorable dogs. When not weaving stories or drawing, she can be found sipping on coffee and expressing her love for toast and Rahman's music.

You can reach her at www.doodleodrama.com

www.ingramcontent.com/pod-product-compliance
Ingram Content Group UK Ltd.
Pitfield, Milton Keynes, MK11 3LW, UK
UKHW060404300726
14090UKWH00006B/428

* 9 7 9 8 8 9 6 7 3 7 5 5 1 *